Teaching the iStudent

CORWIN CONNECTED EDUCATORS SERIES

Teaching the iStudent

A Quick Guide to Using Mobile Devices and Social Media in the K–12 Classroom

Mark Barnes

@markbarnes19

CORWIN
A SAGE Company

CORWIN
A SAGE Company

FOR INFORMATION:

Corwin
A SAGE Company
2455 Teller Road
Thousand Oaks, California 91320
(800) 233-9936
www.corwin.com

SAGE Publications Ltd.
1 Oliver's Yard
55 City Road
London EC1Y 1SP
United Kingdom

SAGE Publications India Pvt. Ltd.
B 1/I 1 Mohan Cooperative Industrial Area
Mathura Road, New Delhi 110 044
India

SAGE Publications Asia-Pacific Pte. Ltd.
3 Church Street
#10-04 Samsung Hub
Singapore 049483

Printed in the United States of America

A catalog record of this book is available from the Library of Congress.

ISBN 978-1-4833-7179-5

This book is printed on acid-free paper.

Executive Editor: Arnis Burvikovs
Associate Editor: Ariel Price
Production Editor: Amy Schroller
Copy Editor: Janet Ford
Typesetter: C&M Digitals (P) Ltd.
Proofreader: Penny Sippel
Cover and Interior Design: Janet Kiesel
Marketing Manager: Lisa Lysne

SUSTAINABLE FORESTRY INITIATIVE
Certified Chain of Custody
Promoting Sustainable Forestry
www.sfiprogram.org
SFI-01268

SFI label applies to text stock

14 15 16 17 18 10 9 8 7 6 5 4 3 2 1

Contents

Preface

Welcome to the Connected Educators Series.

The past few years have provided momentous changes for educators: Whether it's the implementation of the Common Core State Standards, educational innovations due to technology, teacher and administrator evaluations, or budget cuts, what is clear is that educational reforms come in different shapes and sizes. For many connected educators, one of the invaluable group support systems essential during these times is the professional learning network, also known as our PLN.

Our PLN can provide innovative ideas, current resources, and sound educational practices that stretch our thinking in ways we haven't yet experienced. Equally as important as how a PLN can professionally expand our horizons, it introduces new friends that we look forward to meeting in person. This Connected Educator Series brings together some important members of my PLN. These are educators with a depth of knowledge and level of experience that helps me stay current and up-to-date with my educational practices.

In this series, my book, *Flipping Leadership Doesn't Mean Reinventing the Wheel,* takes the innovative idea of flipping classrooms and presents it at the school leader level, engaging the school community in new and innovative ways. In *Connected Leadership,* Spike Cook shares his experiences moving from a novice to digital leadership and illustrates how other educators can do the same.

Digital experts, Steven Anderson and Tom Whitby, help increase your digital experience by using Twitter to locate a PLN to engage in daily professional development. In *The Relevant Educator,* Tom and Steven provide a plethora of tools to use, and define each and every one. Using those same tools, in their book *The Power of Branding,* Tony Sinanis and Joe Sanfelippo help you to brand your school in order to create a positive focus on the learning happening within the four walls. In his book, *All Hands on Deck,* Brad Currie offers us ways to engage with families and students using old techniques with new innovative approaches.

In *Teaching the iStudent,* Mark Barnes provides insight into the life and mind of the iStudent, and in *Empowered Schools, Empowered Students,* Pernille Ripp focuses on em**power**ing students and teachers. Also in the series, in *Diversity and Connected Learning,* Rafranz Davis shows how equity and diversity is vital to the social media movement, and why that is so important to education as we move forward.

Kristen Swanson from the Edcamp Foundation not only focuses on why the Edcamp model is a new innovative way to provide excellent professional development, but also explains how you can create an Edcamp in your school district in *The Edcamp Model: Powering Up Professional Learning.*

The books in the Connected Educator Series are designed to read in any order, and each provides information on the tools that will keep us current in the digital age. We also look forward to continuing the series with more books from experts on connectedness.

As Michael Fullan has said for many years, technology is not the right driver, good pedagogy is. The books in this connected series focus on practices that lead to good pedagogy in our digital age. To assist readers in their connected experience, we created the Corwin Connected Educators companion website (www.corwin .com/connectededucator) where readers can connect with the authors and find resources to help further their experience. It is our hope and intent to meet you where you are in your digital journey, and elevate you as educators to the next level.

Peter M. DeWitt, EdD @PeterMDeWitt

Acknowledgments

Because of a very innovative project a long time ago, I want to acknowledge some amazing minds and awesome former colleagues who inspired parts of this book. To Jennifer Hartz, Riley Parke, Paul Frankmann and Paula Morgan, thanks for opening up the world of web-based learning to me and to our students. Those were the good old days.

Bob Bell, thanks for all of the conversations about best practices in the classroom. You always help me focus when things are blurry.

Peter DeWitt and Arnis Burvikovs, thanks for making me part of this unique series about connected educators.

Ariel Price, thanks for answering every question with patience and professionalism. Without you, I can't imagine this project coming together.

Kathy Cassidy, thanks for all your help and for sharing your amazing students with the world. You and they are game changers.

Aviva Dunsiger, thanks for allowing my readers and me to have a look inside your classroom—a place where learning is truly fun.

To all friends in my Personal Learning Network (far too many to name here), thanks for sharing everyday. Without you, this book wouldn't exist.

About the Author

 **Mark Barnes** is a veteran classroom teacher, international presenter, and author of the critically acclaimed *Role Reversal: Achieving Uncommonly Excellent Results in the Student-Centered Classroom* and *The 5-Minute Teacher: How do I maximize time for learning in my classroom* (Barnes, 2013a, b). Mark is the creator of the internationally recognized how-to video site for teachers, learnitin5.com, and the popular education blog, brilliant-insane.com. Mark tweets at the handle @markbarnes19.

*For Mollie, my loving wife and Ethan and Lauren,
my beautiful children.*

I love you more with every word I write.

Introduction

The eighth-grade classroom was abuzz. Students wandered about, giggling and shouting things like, "Did you see what Jessie wrote?" and "Oh, I read *The Hunger Games* trilogy, too," and "Hey Luke, respond to my last text!" Another student nervously called to the teacher, "Mr. Barnes, I didn't mean to write that; can I delete it?" Still another hollered, "This is awesome. Can we keep the chat going when we leave?" Imagine middle school students wanting to continue an activity outside of class, in essence, asking their teacher for homework. What prompted this excitement, followed by the strange request for additional work? The answer has little to do with the activity or the teacher. This almost uncanny enthusiasm was sparked by the vehicle to learning—the web tool and mobile application called *Celly*.

Just a few years ago, this interactive classroom discussion would have looked quite different. Most likely, students were seated in rows, waiting to be called on by the teacher. The reality then was that most of the class was left out of the discussion completely, as many reluctant learners sat idly by, while their peers carried the session. Even if the discussion or chat was designed as a small-group activity, many students chose to allow others to talk, and the effectiveness of the discussion was lost.

The application, *Celly*, changes everything. Students use computers, tablets, iPods and even smartphones to participate in one of their favorite pastimes—texting. However rather than discuss their latest crush or their exploits on the football field, these Internet-savvy teens eagerly analyze books they've read as part of an independent reading project. The 21st-century learner has become the iStudent—preferring to use the iPod, iPad, iPhone or virtually any other device with Internet capability and a library of applications to remain engaged throughout the day. From very early ages, students wake up to their devices. They are consumed with text messaging, face-timing, downloading apps, and playing games. Rarely, though, do they spend time on their devices learning, because so many school administrators and teachers are still rooted in traditional teaching and learning methods and fear losing control. "The argument is: Cell phones in the classroom mean that students are not paying attention 100 percent" (Klock, 2011). It is this type of belief that makes it difficult for many teachers to encourage the use of mobile devices and social media in their classrooms.

Walk into a progressive school, and you may see students on tablet computers or smartphones, reading, surfing the Internet or even applying an equation to a science project. A decade or two ago, this looked more like a scene from a Star Trek episode than a 21st-century classroom. Even in the early 2000s, when the iPhone, iPad and other tablet computers first

> Even though 1-to-1 schools (one computer per student), cloud computing and mobile learning are becoming popular around the world, sadly, many school districts and their employees have only scratched the surface of understanding the power and importance of digital learning.

appeared on the public's technology radar, most educators could not fathom digital learning as it currently exists. Even though 1-to-1 schools (one computer per student), cloud computing, and mobile learning are becoming popular around the world, sadly, many school districts and their employees have only scratched the surface of understanding the power and importance of digital learning.

Conversely, most of today's students find it difficult to comprehend a universe without the Internet; many cringe at the thought of a day away from their mobile devices. Our students' iPods, smartphones, tablets and eReaders are as much a part of their school gear as paper, pencil, and backpack. For some, the former have completely replaced the latter. Whether downloading an article assigned by a teacher or playing a game retrieved from an app store, these are today's iStudents, and it's time for educators to become iTeachers.

Corwin's Connected Educator series is designed to provide teachers with a roadmap to efficient teaching, learning, and leading in 21st-century schools. The books cover professional development, social networking, community involvement and more, while using technology that empowers all of education's stakeholders. *Teaching the iStudent* is intended to help teachers understand what today's learners know (and don't know), about social media, digital content curation, and mobile learning. Many educators assume that modern students are experts with digital learning tools when, in fact, the opposite is true in most cases. Whether they realize it or not, today's students are tomorrow's content curators and their teachers must help them responsibly create, maintain, and share content. This book provides a philosophical backdrop for connected education, and offers an array of examples of what content curation with social media and mobile learning devices looks like in the 21st-century classroom. Hopefully, it provides you with a go-to manual for advice, technology information, and resources that make you a more effective educator in this age of the iStudent.

CHAPTER

1

Understanding
the Age of "i"

If there is technological advance without social advance,
there is, almost automatically an increase in human misery.

—*Michael Harrington, American writer and theorist*

T he speed of the technology evolution is nearly impossible
to fully comprehend. Recall for a moment the world without social media. No Facebook, Twitter, Instagram, or Pinterest.
How did you keep up with the daily routines of family and
friends? Where did you get your news? The answer to both questions is word of mouth or telephone and newspapers, magazines,
or television. Now, go one step further. Think back to life without a smartphone or, even more incredulous, a simple cell
phone, designed only for calls and text messages. (If you are in
your early 20s, this may be impossible.)

In the past 20 years, society has evolved from a basic cellular phone (the early models weighed about two pounds), to the Internet-ready Blackberry, to today's smartphones complete with nearly one million applications (apps), amazing cameras, video calls, thumbprint security, and more music than we could possibly listen to in a lifetime. When my son was born, I captured his first steps with a fairly small video camera that recorded movies onto a 2.5-inch DVD (digital video disc). That very high tech camcorder cost $900. Today, I record family picnics, upload the video to YouTube and share it with friends and family on Facebook, while maintaining it for posterity in a folder on the cloud-based library, Dropbox. The entire project takes about four minutes, using my iPhone. Just ten years ago, this would have seemed like science fiction. To today's learners, it's a simple routine that many have been doing since about age five—at least the video part.

To truly grasp how rapidly technology evolves, reflect on the fact that the previous video-sharing example will likely be archaic in a few short years. The validity of that statement serves to underscore what educators face when teaching the iStudent. Consider for a moment how you teach and the materials you use. Answer these four questions:

1. How often is paper and pencil part of your class routine?

2. Do your students use workbooks?

3. What role does the Internet play in your classroom?

4. How often do your students use web tools, social media, or mobile devices?

Although there is certainly a relationship between the four questions, the latter two are the focal questions in this book.

The iStudent, beginning in about third grade, walks into school with some kind of device, whether it's an iPod or other music player, a smartphone, an eReader or, in rare cases, just some type of headphones. In one way or another, virtually every one of your students is connected to the Internet, an application, and social media. Yet, many schools are so caught up in standardization and testing that they continue to ignore the iStudent's need to be connected. As a result, the bridge between these infinitely powerful tools and genuine learning remains at best tenuous, and at worst completely crumbled. As a 20-year classroom teacher, and now full-time consultant working with educators around the world, it is my experience that the average teacher and school administrator fail to fully grasp the needs of the iStudent.

In what can aptly be called the "age of i," society has become dependent on technology, in general, and on electronic gadgets, in particular. The aforementioned disconnect between technology and learning is a threefold issue caused by:

1. A school's or district's Acceptable Use Policy (AUP)

2. Educators' inexperience with using the technology for teaching and learning

3. Students' misunderstanding of how to appropriately use the technology at their fingertips for learning

The first problem may preclude the second: if teachers are unable to access the necessary technology, then the experience becomes difficult to acquire, and for all intents and purposes, obsolete; as educators are blocked from using websites and mobile learning tools, they have no reason to understand them—at least when related to their positions at school. Although I certainly have recommendations for the first issue, chiefly educating school policymakers about the value of the technology and about appropriate classroom use—it is poorly written AUPs that often make teaching the iStudent nearly impossible. This is when many effective teachers resort to traditional methods, like worksheets, text questions, and multiple-choice tests. Assuming your district has progressive policies that encourage mobile learning devices and lenient network firewalls that don't block the majority of useful websites, the second previously mentioned problem with disconnected educators becomes imminently important. All 21st-century teachers must educate themselves on the tools of the iStudent, prior to dealing with the third issue—teaching those students how to efficiently use the Internet and their technology gadgets for the purpose of learning. The following sections investigate what is most important for the iStudent to learn, as well as how teachers can maximize digital learning in their classrooms. Along the way, the three issues outlined in this chapter are answered more thoroughly.

Content Curation in the 21st Century

You are what you share.

—*C.W. Leadbeater, prominent*
theosophist and author

At the risk of exaggeration, let me begin this chapter by saying that understanding content curation may be the most important part of 21st-century education. The word "curation," and its derivatives, does not appear in the Common Core State Standards, and I doubt your course of study is littered with objectives about content curation. The reason for this omission most likely is that curation has only become a big part of digital learning parlance within the past couple of years; however, the notion that content curation is an integral part of teaching and learning is rapidly gaining traction. Author Judy O'Connell in a 2012 blog post titled *Educators as Content Curators* wrote,

> Searching for content requires wise information literacy strategies and tools (embedded in the curriculum learning processes) to avoid being lost in the information labyrinth. Content curation is also about organizing, filtering and 'making sense of' information on the web and sharing the very best pieces of content that has been selected for a specific purpose or need. (p. 1)

> Although using an app store certainly has value, locating the right tools and understanding how to use them for independent learning and content curation is arguably the 21st-century learner's most critical skill and should be part of every educator's weekly lesson plans.

As suggested in O'Connell's essay, educators are beginning to consider how information is created, maintained, and shared and what methods are best for teaching students how to sift through the ocean of content available on social networks, blogs and millions of websites, some legitimate, many dubious.

> Firstly, we need to filter the many and various digital tools and apps available. There are several ways we could do this, but a good way would be to focus on the capacity the technology has to engage, to facilitate learning and to improve children's skills and knowledge for the 21st Century. (Donahoo, 2012, p. 1, para. 2)

WHY CURATION?

In Chapter 1, I noted the three important issues facing teachers of the iStudent. To paraphrase the third, our students are ignorant of the ways to use the amazing tools at their fingertips. Sure, they can play games, which certainly have a valuable role in learning, but when it comes to content curation, even many of the brightest young adults struggle to grasp the power of the information that they create, manage, and share on a daily basis.

For their part, many administrators and teachers today maintain the assumption that students are highly skilled technology users. This is understandable, when young adults enter the room with Internet-ready devices, and they seem to navigate the World Wide Web and app markets as easily as they flip open their textbooks. The problem is that while the so-called digital native—the student who is born in the midst of desktop computers, iPads, and smartphones—may be an expert at downloading games and music, he or she likely has little experience using a social media tool (e.g., Diigo and Twitter), for gathering information, annotating it, and sharing it with teachers and peers. Although using an app store certainly has value, locating the right tools and understanding how to use them for independent learning and content curation is arguably the 21st-century learner's most critical skill and should be part of every educator's weekly lesson plans.

The concept of curation as an invaluable skill can be elusive. As previously mentioned, the term is relatively new, at least when related to digital content. Before we look at the role of mobile learning and other tools that students should be able to manage and use for sharing information, let's flesh out the philosophy of content curation and why it

> We are obligated to teach our students how the information they curate may ultimately define them and may impact innumerable people in their society.

is so meaningful when done right. Students must first understand that the moment they create, locate, and/or share something on the Internet, they are now, in fact, curators, whether they like it or not. Although the word should carry a positive connotation, I always relate it to librarians or art collectors, some of the world's most valued curators, teaching students the deleterious effects of the wrong kind of content curation emphasizes the importance of the word and its significant connotations.

Consider the story of British fourteen-year-old Hannah Smith. A variety of sources reported that Smith committed suicide after being cyber bullied on a social network called, *Ask.fm*. According to a United Kingdom website, theguardian.com: One user said she should "go die, evry1 wuld be happy," another recommended: "do us all a favour n kill ur self." Someone told her "no1 would care if ya died u cretin" (Henley, 2013). Smith was not the first teenager to commit suicide after reading disparaging remarks on an Internet site. She was one of the most recent, though, and her suicide brought negative publicity to *Ask.fm*, prompting company co-founder Mark Terebin to argue that, "*Ask*.fm is just a tool that helps people to communicate, same as any other social network, same as a phone, same as piece of paper and pen. Don't blame a tool" (Henley, 2013). This is similar to the old argument, "It's not guns that kill people. It's people who kill people." Notwithstanding how tantalizing this debate might be, the point is that America has gun laws in place to encourage responsibility. The Hannah Smith story and others like it can be used as a strong foundation for teaching students the responsibility that accompanies creating, sharing, and maintaining information and opinion on the Internet.

This example, of course, puts a fine point on how content curation can be an awful thing. On the flipside, educators must emphasize the incredible power of appropriate curation. Rather than only teaching young people about the dangers of Facebook, Twitter, and Instagram, we must show them what these social media allow us to maintain: a record of events, in both graphic and written formats; the management of an amazing network of people who supply learning opportunities daily; and, possibly most important of all, how to share knowledge.

> Establishing a PLN seems simple enough on the surface, but to do it successfully and optimize its potential contains within it a challenging and vigorous set of learning opportunities. Curating, managing, and promoting a PLN develops critical, creative, 21st century, and an increasingly important set of socio-emotional capabilities. (Moss, 2013, p. 1, para. 4)

We are obligated to teach our students how the information they curate may ultimately define them and may impact innumerable people in their society. Curation is an important element throughout the remainder of this book; consider its implications on everything you plan to do from this point forward.

CHAPTER
3

Why You Can't Afford to Ignore Social Media

Social media spark a revelation that we, the people, have a voice, and through the democratization of content and ideas we can once again unite around common passions, inspire movements, and ignite change.

—*Brian Solis, digital analyst and author*

Remember the sad story of Hannah Smith? Some might argue that she fell victim to social media. As I emphasize in the prior chapter, this is also a curation issue, because students fail to understand the power and posterity of what they create, maintain, and share and how ill-conceived and haphazardly shared content can be damaging to many parties. It's abundantly clear that social media is a force that entices our students. Recent research indicates that 95 percent of students, between the ages of 12 and 17, use the Internet and 81 percent frequent some sort of social media site (Sterling, 2013). The average teen Facebook user reports having roughly 425 Facebook friends (Sterling, 2013). These are remarkably influential people, regardless of their age or professional status (if they have one).

The teens of today may be ignorant of many worldly and academic things, and may not fully comprehend the impact of social media, but they appear to know the source of their most relevant information. Many schools are beginning to model social media use. It is not uncommon for school districts to have Facebook and Twitter accounts. They are sharing school and student news with parents and the community and alerting their stakeholders to key events, such as upcoming football games, school closings, and other events using social networks.

It's important for educators to realize that students are following in our footsteps. They, too, are using Facebook, Twitter, Instagram, Pinterest, Vine, and unfortunately, sites like *Ask.fm* to share content. Harkening back to the chapter on curation, educators are now faced with the daunting responsibility of teaching our students how to use social media to appropriately manage content. So, how do we do it? There are several important steps to ensure that students use social networks as tools for good rather than as a means for bullying others, or simply talking about the big upcoming dance.

TEAR DOWN THE FIREWALLS

It is time for schools to stop blocking Facebook, Twitter, Instagram and other social networks that students love and already use daily outside of school. The upcoming section on mobile learning examines the invaluable role of electronic devices in class. Assuming teachers begin using these amazing tools, it's equally important to embrace the social networks, which can also be engaging platforms for teaching and learning. For some teachers, this is like saying, "Hold your hand over this flame; everything will be all right." It's nearly impossible to envision the combination of social media and learning, without getting burned. This is because teachers, by their very nature, are on high alert; we want to keep our students safe. Of course, when it comes to social media, we tend to immediately assume the worst.

Stories like the one about Hannah Smith make this understandable, perhaps even reasonable. In order to overcome this fear, students must be allowed to access social networks in class, so they are given the opportunity to misuse the medium and then hopefully learn to successfully and appropriately use this wondrous technology. Education technology expert Doug Johnson deftly underscores the danger of limiting student access to social media:

> If Facebook, Twitter and the like are blocked from student access, the foray into this astonishing universe of digital collaboration cannot begin.

It's true that the world of Internet 2.0 can be dangerous. But there is also a genuine, if not as immediate or well-publicized, danger in preventing students from accessing the tools they need to participate in collaborative online learning experiences, to communicate with global experts and fellow students, and to collect data and do research. (Johnson, 2014, p. 1, para. 11)

Working globally sounds amazing, indeed. However, if Facebook, Twitter and the like are blocked from student access, the foray into this astonishing universe of digital collaboration cannot begin. Getting there has to be a team effort. Teachers, principals, superintendents, parents and even students must work together to create an action plan for appropriate use.

IF YOU BUILD IT, THEY WILL LEARN

Chapter 7 identifies many terms and abbreviations that help with successful technology integration. One is AUP, or Acceptable Use Policy. Having an AUP and teaching appropriate technology use are two very different things. It's a fair assumption that by reading this book, you're taking the first step toward creating a technology-rich environment that engages today's iStudent. The next step is to begin teaching appropriate use of computers, tablets, handheld devices, headphones, and certainly, the Internet and social media.

Teaching and reviewing appropriate use must begin on Day 1 and continue throughout the school year—every school year. Unless students have been using social media in prior years at your school, the first time you tell them to go to Facebook or Twitter, they will be shocked. Of course, your worst fears may come true. They'll want to look at a friend's pages or tweets, which may contain content that is inappropriate for your classroom. Use this as a teachable moment. Instead of shielding them from the content, discuss why it can't be viewed at school. Set specific boundaries for social media and Internet use. Explain the kinds of searches that are appropriate and those that are not. For example, a search for "swimsuit" most likely results in many pages of scantily clad models. "But, this is what they wear on the beach," an eager student may justify. Again, think teachable moment. Your class is not the beach, and many things that may seem okay outside of school are not okay in your classroom.

> Constant reinforcement of appropriate use will create a symbiotic relationship between the technology and how students use it, and this will forever serve them well.

When I used social media for learning in class, the boundaries were clear. We could search for any information that was topical, using only specific search terms. Posting to Facebook, Instagram, or Twitter was not allowed, unless we were using a social network to have a class conversation. In other words, a Twitter chat, with a specific topic-related hashtag, requires posting tweets. In this case, everyone in the classroom, including me and any invited adult (e.g., administrators or parents), can see exactly what students are posting. (You learn more about hashtags in Chapter 7.) When students understand boundaries and appropriate use, they almost always do the right thing, because they enjoy the technology and don't want to risk losing it. Just remember to teach and reteach appropriate use constantly. Encourage discussion and debate on the subject. Appropriate use should become as omnipresent as the devices and social networks that the students use. Constant reinforcement of appropriate use creates a symbiotic relationship between the technology and how students use it, and this will forever serve them well.

Ramp up Lessons with Social Media

As much as I say that school and learning should be fun, teachers obviously have to meet objectives and ensure that learning takes place. The "old school" methods made this easy; just hand out a workbook designed to teach concepts and skills, and hope the lesson sinks in. This kind of teaching is simple, but it rarely stimulates any sort of critical thinking, and the learning is, at best, questionable. While it's easy to envision how using the Internet and social media as teaching tools could make learning fun, it's far more challenging to integrate learning outcomes, while using these interactive perks. This is where intense planning is required.

As with any good lesson, start planning by beginning at the end— the objective. What do you want your students to learn? Let's assume you're using the following Common Core State Standard for sixth-grade math: "Apply and extend previous understandings of multiplication and division to divide fractions by fractions. . . For example, create a story context for 2/3 divided by 3/4 and use a visual fraction model to show the quotient" (National Governors Association, 2010, p. 42). This is a perfect opportunity to use a social network to not only tell the story, but to converse about it with peers and with the teacher. A classroom Facebook page might work well for this example. Another option is to blend the learning (more on this later), and have students work on the problem on paper, followed by a Twitter chat using the hashtag, #fractionmodel. Mind you, I've never taught math and, in fact, struggle to help my fifth-grade son with it, but it's easy to see in this example how a skilled math teacher could engage students in learning about fractions with this type of activity. Remember, often it isn't the activity that is the key to student engagement as much as the tool that is used. If your students learn more using Facebook, Twitter, or Instagram, why fight that battle? The ultimate goal is that students learn.

I could recite a wide array of examples using science, social studies, and even Health/PE (i.e., post pictures to Instagram demonstrating the effects of steroids on the body, and tweet them to the classroom Twitter account), but I'm certain you now understand how easy this approach can be. Decide on your learning outcome, consider which social media tool works best for the assignment, name the activity or project, and then experience and enjoy student engagement like you've never seen it before.

Unless you are teaching very young children, there is little doubt that your students are using social media. They are creating, managing, and sharing content, and most assuredly this will be the case for the foreseeable future.

In order to avoid tragedies like Hannah Smith, and since social networks can also be powerful teaching and learning platforms, it's crucial that educators embrace them and teach students how to use them appropriately. For schools to ignore social media may ultimately harm students in multiple ways.

Start When They're Young

Copyright © Kathy Cassidy

When I discuss social media for teaching and learning at education conferences and workshops, most attendees love the idea. Invariably, the biggest skeptics are the elementary teachers. "I teach first grade," someone chimes in, head shaking vigorously from left to right. "My kids can't use Twitter." I have to admit to thoroughly enjoying these moments and even breaking into a wry smile, before responding, "Hmm, are you certain about that?" Then, I share a video of Kathy Cassidy's first graders explaining how they learn using Twitter. Cassidy, author of *Connected from the Start: Global Learning in the Primary Grades* (Cassidy, 2013), created a classroom Twitter page, @mscassidysclass so that all of her six-year-olds could sign into the same account without registering for the site. When students tweet, they simply add their name at the end, so their peers and teacher can connect their words back to them. "What began as a way to connect with parents has become a place for us to connect with other classrooms or experts and a place for my students to learn together," Cassidy writes in an e-mail. "We use Twitter to show our own learning, such as when we tweet using the "voice" of Red Riding Hood's wolf, to learn

serendipitously from the tweets of others and above all, to learn to read and write."

Thus, Twitter becomes a powerful content curation tool while providing a platform for very young students to learn appropriate use of a social network. As Cassidy's e-mail aptly summarizes, "Twitter is an engaging and succinct way for students to express themselves. It shares their learning with an authentic audience and teaches important digital skills."

Although there is no hard evidence to support this claim, it seems obvious that if we teach students when they are very young how to use social media appropriately, they are more likely to use it efficiently and appropriately as they grow older. Kathy Cassidy's first graders are a prime example of how elementary students can engage in 21st-century content curation using social media. It is difficult to dispute the assertion that Cassidy's six-year-olds will be more prepared to manage content and engage worldwide audiences on social media than their peers, who spend the bulk of their days using pencil and paper. Remember, iStudents are young students; hone their social media skills as soon as they begin to read and write.

CHAPTER
4

How Mobile Learning
Changes Everything

Mobile phones are misnamed. They should be called gateways to human knowledge.

—*Ray Kurzweil, author, scientist, inventor, futurist*

I n 2011, a lifetime ago in the digital age, important studies began revealing the power of mobile learning. The Pew Internet and American Life Project was already touting the impact of Internet and social media "connectivity," saying that because of small devices, new kinds of learners were emerging (Rainie, 2011, slide 3). Several years later, the ubiquity of these "small devices" has increased exponentially. In July of 2012, 58 percent of teens, ages 13 to 17 had a smartphone, an increase of 60 percent from the prior year (Meredith, 2012, page 1, para. 2). Consider this increase for a moment. If the number of teens owning a smartphone increased an eye-popping 60 percent in a 12-month span, how long will it take before every teenage student has a smartphone? It is plausible that before this decade ends, all students, even many in elementary schools, will have a smartphone or a similar Internet-ready device. Can educators continue to ignore these statistics and the possibilities that accompany them? Moreover, can we remain steadfast in dust-laden policies that instruct students to leave their devices in lockers, or worse, at home?

> It's time for educators and school policymakers to stop ignoring their most important stakeholders.

If this data isn't enough, consider how students feel about mobile learning. In a recent national study of students' attitudes toward mobile devices, including elementary, middle, and high school students, an astonishing 92 percent reported believing that tablets will change the way students learn in the future, and a whopping 96 percent of elementary students said tablets make learning fun (Harris Interactive, 2013). It's time for educators and school policymakers to stop ignoring their most important stakeholders. In order to maximize digital learning in the classroom, educators must acknowledge that mobile learning devices are not going away. Instead of demanding that students put them in their pockets, purses, or lockers, we should be telling students to bring their devices to class and to set them on their tabletops.

Another critical consideration when it comes to teaching the iStudent is the direction learning is headed, based on the omnipresence of social media and open-source learning tools, as well as the previously mentioned lightning fast adoption of mobile devices by students. There is a large contingent of education philosophers who believe that Massively Open Online Courses, or MOOCs, are a new wave that may one day consume brick and mortar schools. Although I doubt that you are running off to rework your resume in fear that your teaching career is headed for certain demise, it is worth noting that free online courses, currently aimed only at college-level students, are gaining traction among many scholars.

> MOOCs in their strict, literal sense have relatively limited potential primarily as branding for institutions and individual professors. . . Do they have the potential to be more? Lots of people think so, including a group of professors at Harvard, in direct response to California system professors who have objected. (Mitrano, 2013, para. 1)

Why is this information important for teaching the iStudent and for this chapter on mobile learning? The main reason is to underscore the power of online learning. It is possible today to take an entire college course from a smartphone or tablet. Secondly, if this is a future possibility for our current K–12 students, then it is crucial that teachers prepare them for this eventuality, before they graduate from high school. Without embracing mobile devices and some sort of blended learning approach, it's quite possible that our students will lack the necessary skills to take advantage of the independent learning opportunities that MOOCs and other open source Internet tools provide.

WHAT CHANGE LOOKS LIKE

Recall the scene in the introduction, when students were engaged in a stimulating conversation, using the text messaging website and mobile app, Celly (www.cell.ly). When I began using Celly in my classroom, most teachers at my school feared this type of activity. Students were typically instructed to leave any type of electronic device in their lockers. While trying to respect my school's policies as much as possible, this was a time when I knew that bending those rules was necessary. I had a group of reluctant learners, and I needed to engage them any way that I could. When reluctant learners see their teacher as a bit of a rebel, this perception can go a long way to earning their respect (Barnes, 2013a). So, telling them to bring their cell phones to class so we can text each other immediately got their attention.

Engaging students with applications and social media like Celly, Twitter, and Facebook is easy, because the iStudent is always ready to jump on a computer, tablet or mobile device; it's in his or her nature. However, the key to successful integration for learning is teaching students how to not only have fun, but how to apply the technology to the learning outcome.

One key ingredient to successful technology integration is not forgetting the autonomy and the fun. When I first exposed my students to our classroom website, barnesclass.com, they were amazed at the interactivity that it presented. As they built their own private websites, complete with the ability to create multiple pages, links, and to add pictures, music, and videos, they became more inspired. "Put pictures on your home page," I said. "Add some color and maybe some information about you. Have fun with it, because it's yours." Their first reaction was shock. It was rare for a teacher to tell them to make their own choices and to have fun with what they knew was a tool for learning. Given the freedom to create something unique, they wanted to visit their web pages and, along the way, spend time on our classroom website, because they believed they had built something that was truly their own.

Subsequently, we began using the website for learning. Brief video instruction introduced the concepts and skills students needed to apply to other activities and projects. When the videos ended, students would race off to their private classroom web pages to create something that demonstrated what they'd learned. I can't emphasize enough the importance of that first experience with a new digital learning tool or device. If my students were told to go to their new web pages and analyze the plot in a short story they read, they would have almost certainly looked on the classroom website as nothing more than digital pencil and paper, and the learning would have suffered. Similarly, when first introduced to Celly, students wasted little time texting fun messages to their peers and even to me. "Hey, Mr. Barnes, texting is not allowed in school" was my favorite. Rather than barking at them that the program is for learning and threatening to ban them if they didn't keep their texts topical, I simply joined the fun. "I won't tell, if you don't," I replied to the student's quip about texting being against the rules. This received a host of giggles around the room, and the students embraced Celly as a fun way to learn. When the texting shifted back to the class topic, the transition was smooth. As long as time for the fun texts is built in, the ones that demonstrated reading comprehension seamlessly filled in the gaps.

So, remember that when using a web tool or mobile application, don't leap immediately to objectives or skills. Instead, in order for the mobile learning to be effective, first encourage your students to explore the technology the same way they explore the games and music that they download to their devices everyday. Afterwards, explain how they can use the tool to demonstrate their under-standing of the content and skills you are teaching and they need to learn. Remind them that boundaries do exist; there are times when deviating from the lesson is not acceptable. As long as you give them time to use technology for fun, students rarely abuse it.

HOLSTER THAT LESSON PLAN

Often, teachers are so consumed with standards, learning out-comes, and courses of study that they fear giving up too much time to digital learning activities. I find that occasionally provid-ing a break from instruction, so students can use technology any way they wish (within the boundaries of class), is a powerful way to encourage focus at other times. In *The 5-Minute Teacher: How do I maximize time for learning in my classroom*, I call this a "Tech Timeout" (Barnes, 2013b). I tell students that this doesn't mean a timeout from technology; instead, it is a break from class work. This helps reinforce the boundary that is necessary for effective use of the Internet and of mobile devices. Because they expect to have some downtime that they can enjoy in any way they like, students are much more willing to return to the learning. In fact, when your digital learning activities are truly engaging, you may find that many students ignore your Tech Timeout completely and elect to continue the current activity or project for the class.

You're Not an Expert. So What?

You can see more of what mobile learning in the classroom looks like in Chapter 6. Meanwhile, if you are concerned that you don't know enough about the mobile devices and social networks that the iStudent loves, build your own network of professionals to help increase your knowledge and skills. Twitter, Facebook and other social networks are rife with educators, who are remarkably knowledgeable about digital learning. You might consider starting with the authors of the Connected Educator series. Follow them on Twitter and read their blogs. You can find information about all of them on the Connected Educators companion website. Don't be afraid to reach out and ask for help—that is what being connected is all about.

CHAPTER
5

Blending the Learning

> Blended learning has the potential to upend today's factory-model school system, which standardizes the way it teaches and tests, and instead enable personalized learning approaches for all students.
>
> —*Michael Horn, author and digital advocate*

It is unfair to suggest that most educators are anti-digital devices. In fact, I've worked with teachers nationwide who love the idea of mobile learning. In most cases, the problem is that many teachers are not anti-device, they simply don't have the experience or the training necessary to implement a successful mobile learning strategy. Teachers at education conferences and at schools often admit that they struggle with striking a balance between a more traditional teaching approach—which generally involves textbooks, workbooks, homework and tests—and using technology. "I want my kids to use their devices," is commonly heard, "but how do I do that and complete our weekly workbook pages?" This is a conundrum, to say the least. At the risk of appearing brazen, my first suggestion is to eliminate the workbook pages entirely. As indicated in studies and anecdotes shared earlier, iStudents are far more interested in learning on the Internet and on their mobile devices. Of course, many schools are not yet ready to discard their workbook programs, even though this move could save tens of thousands of dollars and spark far more interest in learning.

So, if the traditional approaches remain intact in your school, then what you should consider adopting is a successful "blended learning" approach. Combining face-to-face learning with technology integration and web-based instruction creates a blended learning environment. To clarify, imagine a science class that begins with brief direct instruction about cellular mitosis. Students can read about mitosis in a textbook and take notes based on the text and/ or the teacher's direct instruction. At this point, depending on the class environment, students could move to computers, tablets, or their own mobile devices and view a YouTube video demonstrating mitosis (of course, the video could be shown on an interactive whiteboard). The remainder of the activity is triggered based on the blended approach the teacher selects. There are a variety of blended learning programs, and each depends on your environment and your students' needs. A few of these blended learning approaches are discussed in the remainder of this chapter.

Rotation Model

Years ago, I worked in a classroom that had four desktop computers. When you have 25 to 30 students, it is difficult to efficiently use such limited technology. I'm ashamed to admit that I once told a principal that my class was better off without the computers since they only served to distract the students. Of course, this was before I understood how to blend the learning. Thankfully, I kept the computers and employed a blended learning rotation model. In this approach, students rotate to computer stations in groups. The teacher provides direct instruction to one group, while others work collaboratively or independently and another group of students works on a technology-driven activity or project. If your class is limited to just a few computers, as mine was, encourage students to use their mobile devices as well. With some clever group management, you can easily have eight to 10 students on a computer. After a set amount of time, all students rotate to the next station. The benefits of this model are that it creates multiple transitions between activities engaging students and making class time appear to move more quickly. Concurrently, this model also maximizes use of resources for classes that are limited to only a few computers.

Flex Model

If your class is equipped with many computers, or if your school embraces a Bring Your Own Device (BYOD) policy, students spend a bulk of their class time on a technology-driven activity or project while the teacher takes on the coaching role, moving from student to student for more individualized and small group instruction. The flex model creates a student-centered classroom where learning is more interactive and students are more engaged.

> Instruction is blended in the flex format when students leave the technology periodically, so they can interact with their teacher and with friends.

This model allows a skillful teacher easy differentiation of instruction, and multiple learning opportunities for groups and individuals, depending on their skills and understanding of material. For example, if using a classroom blog or Facebook page, you might ask one group of students to compare two pieces of classic literature and comment on each other's posts. For a group that is struggling with the content, you might ask these students to break down a single chapter, identifying key characters and the conflicts they face. All students are engaged on a digital learning platform, without realizing that they are completing different activities. The flex model also provides plenty of time to converse with individuals, and facilitates coaching, formative assessment, and rapport building.

Aviva Dunsiger, who teaches 5th graders in Ontario, Canada, makes excellent use of multiple blended learning models, including the flex approach. During many personal conversations with her, she explains that her students use various social networks and websites to enhance in-class activities. Dunsiger says her students "learn alongside experts online while also interacting with their peers, face-to-face, in the classroom. For example, this year, after finishing our science unit on the human body, we saw that Sunnybrook Hospital was live tweeting a heart surgery. Students followed the tweets and responded to the doctor with questions and comments of their own."

Copyright © Aviva Dunsiger

Instruction is blended in the flex format when students leave the technology periodically, so they can interact with their teacher and with friends. "They could discuss their thoughts with their peers in the classroom, while also learning more through the tweet responses that we received," Dunsiger explains. "The doctor even offered to Skype with our class during a lunch hour (the following week) and answer additional questions. Blended learning brought this science learning to a whole new level, as students got to apply what they learned, engage in more meaningful discussions with each other as they tweeted, and learn from an outside expert as well."

Lab Model

Some classes are driven by online learning modules or textbook supplement programs. In these cases, one or more days may be spent in computer labs or in classrooms with mobile laptop carts. In a lab setting, students usually work on a prefabricated tutorial program or class project for the bulk of the time. The lab is typically more conducive to independent activities or online evaluations, but it can be used for web-based projects and/or collaboration, if coached properly. The main benefit of the lab model is the change of environment, which most students enjoy. Like the constant transition in the rotation model, moving to the computer lab several times weekly often motivates students to remain focused while in the traditional classroom. The key is not to threaten taking the computer lab away as a consequence for disruption; rather, remind students that they need to reach a particular point during class activities, so they are ready to work efficiently on lab days. Computer labs also give students a time to focus on their own progress within the confines of their individual computer or web-based program. The teacher continues to act as more of a coach, much as in the flex model.

Connecting in the Blended Classroom

Although the demise of the brick and mortar school in favor of MOOCs and similar options may be on the horizon, at least for now using blended learning presents students with the best of both worlds. "Technology allows us to connect with other classrooms and learn together," Dunsiger says of this powerful new education frontier. "Social media makes classroom learning about more than just what's happening in the four walls of the classroom: the whole world can learn along with us!" Some direct teacher contact is still important, as is collaboration with peers. Students faced with sitting quietly in rows of desks, filling in blanks in workbooks for 45 minutes at a time, become restless and bored. Conversely, when promised the opportunity to mix seatwork with collaboration and digital learning, they become inspired. So, consider your students' needs and your classroom environment, and decide which model is most efficient for you and your students. Now, all you need is an activity and a web tool or application, and tomorrow might just open up that world that Dunsiger's students regularly experience.

CHAPTER 6

Activities and Tools You Can Use Tomorrow

We can't solve problems by using the same kind of thinking we used when we created them.

—Albert Einstein, theoretical physicist and genius

Much of this book defines and examines digital learning and the role it plays in the 21st-century classroom. Unless you skipped ahead to this chapter, you should now have plenty of insight into the iStudent. You know that today's learner comes ready to use the Internet, applications, social media, and a wide variety of mobile devices, but he or she may not be an expert at applying these powerful tools to learning. You learned that content curation is how people in today's society create, manage, and share information on both a personal and professional level. You understand the variations possible in blended learning environments and how and why you might choose that particular approach. In this chapter, I share specific examples of numerous types of web tools and applications of tremendous value to the educator and to the iStudent. These tools can be used for presentation, content sharing, collaboration, and even for evaluation.

> Educators often ask me, which one of these platforms is better? The answer is invariably: The one that you and your students are most comfortable using, as long as it completes the desired task.

A critical point of emphasis when considering web tools and apps is that most of the time the chosen tool isn't nearly as important as its use. For example, I like to share content to my social networks with an application called, *Buffer*. Many people prefer to use *Hootsuite* or *Scoop.it*. (You can learn more about these tools at the Connected Educators companion website.) Each of these apps has a similar use—to share content across multiple social networks. In other words, I might find a fabulous blog post about mobile learning that I want to distribute to my friends and followers on Twitter, LinkedIn, and Facebook, and the previously mentioned apps allow me to share this information with a single click. That is powerful content curation, to say the least. Educators often ask me, which one of these platforms is better? The answer is invariably: "The one that you and your students are most comfortable using, as long as it completes the desired task."

In the time it takes you to finish reading this section, you will discover activities, driven by engaging web tools and apps that you can use tomorrow regardless of the grade or subject you teach. Remember, the examples provided are sites and apps I successfully use in my middle school language arts class. You may want a different tool for a similar task, or you may want the same tool for a different task; the key is to consider the learning outcome that you want your students to master. And you can always refer to the companion website for more examples of powerful tools and activities.

PRE- OR POST-WRITING ACTIVITY

Of course, you know about response writing, but if you recall the *Celly* example, it's often not the activity that can inspire students as much as it is the network tool they select. Want your students to start thinking about a topic before your planned instruction? Ask them to write something that they can share to stimulate conversation—an excellent activity. However, if you ask them to write in a notebook, many will decline. Instead, why not have your students write their responses in a blog post?

I have seen students sit down, or worse yet, put their heads down, when I asked the class to answer a question in a written paragraph in notebooks. In fact, with some groups when assigned this activity, it wasn't at all uncommon for five or six out of 20 students to simply do nothing. Then I started using *Kidblog*, a writing platform designed by educators for educators. With *Kidblog*, every student is allocated his or her own blog site, which is contained in the classroom Content Management System. The key here is that all students can read what their peers are writing and, best of all, they can comment on it. You can choose a different blog platform, such as *Google's Blogger*, but then the students' blogs have to be managed with a reader like *Feedly*, which is a news aggregator application that I discuss a little later in this chapter. If you are currently using *Feedly*, you may prefer *Blogger*, as it gives your students even more ownership of their blogs; however, be advised that it does eliminate much of the control that many teachers want and that *Kidblog* provides.

Getting Started. Go to *Kidblog.org* and register your classroom blog for free. In a few short minutes, you'll be ready to engage your students with their own blogs. Use *Kidblog*'s "secret code" function to help register students. This is a truly amazing feature, because you don't have to enter any user information. Students can literally be registered and blogging in about five minutes. Once your students set up their profiles and blog templates, they can begin writing and commenting. Imagine some class days beginning with students heading straight to their computers, tablets, or even their

Kindles or Nooks and typing a blog post on a topic that provokes online discussion. Blogging is also a wonderful way to end a class period or day. It can be an exit ticket or just serve as a journal. *Kidblog* is good for all students in any subject. Best of all, one of the many benefits is that if your students regularly blog, their writing skills significantly increase.

CURATE CONTENT

As noted, if your students are using independent blog platforms like *Blogger*, you may want to add their blogs to a reader like *Feedly*, which makes it easy to organize the content any way that you prefer and you can read your students' articles from anywhere, including your own mobile device. Better still, teach young learners how to use *Feedly*, or similar apps, as powerful tools for content curation. While *Scoop.it*, *Flipboard*, and *Netvibes* are other serviceable choices, I prefer *Feedly* because it is remarkably user-friendly. Once you and your students register, *Feedly* walks you through basic steps to add content from around the Internet. Since this book is so much about content curation, having a go-to application for gathering, maintaining, and sharing information is critical. Even the most reluctant readers search for content, once they know that the handcuffs have been removed, and they can add anything to their Feedly library. Given that reaction, this is an opportune time to reinforce appropriate use. Explain the responsibility of curating appropriate, powerful information, as students will not only find content they like, but they will share it to various social networks through the Feedly app. Tell them that they are literally feeding their brains and the intellects of people all around the world with the content they create (they can add their own blogs to Feedly), locate, and maintain.

Getting started. Guide students to *Feedly.com* and have them register. Then, *Feedly* instructs users to "Organize, read and share what matters to you" above a search box. Your students can search for content with keywords, such as "sports," "fashion" or "books."

Many popular sites will appear and can be added with a simple point and click. In minutes, students are creating libraries of content that say a lot about them and their values. Even the way that they organize blogs and websites into categories is a key part of efficient content curation. Imagine a class period where students add 10 to 20 websites to their *Feedly* libraries and begin sharing articles with their peers via Twitter, using a classroom hashtag that you create. The follow-up lessons to an activity like this are boundless.

Make a Movie

Another tool is *Animoto* (www.animoto.com, an online video maker), and the best part of this application is that students don't need a camera or other people to create amazing movies. *Animoto* comprises both a website platform and iOS and Google applications, meaning that students can use it with computers, laptops, tablets, or their Apple or Android device. *Animoto* provides users with a library of pictures and graphics, plus links to social media with unlimited access to other pictures. Existing pictures and brief videos can also be uploaded to *Animoto*. A science teacher can have students locate various pictures of vertebrates or invertebrates and upload them to *Animoto*, followed by content that explains the pictures. The music library gives students a nice sense of autonomy, as they can decide which melody best fits their movie. Titles and descriptions can be added, and completed 30-second movies can be shared in a variety of ways, including links and embedded codes for transfer to blogs and websites. There are other similar apps, like *Magisto*, which might be preferred by some teachers and students, and you can learn more about these at the Connected Educators companion website.

Getting Started. Show students how to register for *Animoto* for free. Walk them through the features: selecting pictures and videos from various places, adding text boxes, arranging images and content so they tell a story, selecting appropriate music, mixing the final movie, and selecting the method for sharing. Students using the mobile app on a phone or tablet can take pictures or short videos with the device and immediately add them to their *Animoto* movie. This may be more useful, in some cases, than uploading pictures from the web. You will find that similar to *Kidblog*, students love the idea of using *Animoto*. My middle schoolers wanted to use it all of the time for virtually everything. It's easy and fun. Still, don't forget to explain the learning outcome. Students need to know what skill or concept their movie demonstrates. It may take several tries before real learning is visible. Be patient, and spend time coaching the finer points of locating good information for the movies. Remind them that this is content curation—a critical 21st-century skill.

Online Chat

Wouldn't it be wonderful to have every one of your students participate in a class discussion? Yes, that means 100 percent participation. It's easy. Stop asking students to raise their hands. Put them on computers or their mobile devices and have them go to a room you create, using *TodaysMeet*, a realtime, live stream application. This is an activity applicable to any subject and with students at almost any age level. The teacher creates an online room that is secure, because only the teacher and students have the address. Math instructors can have students discuss how they solved a problem or how to apply a skill to a real-world situation. Foreign language teachers might direct students to demonstrate words or phrases they've learned. Health students might discuss the impact of a new study on future cancer diagnosis and/or treatment. *TodaysMeet* allows you to retrieve a script of your conversation and save it for later use. Similar to other web-based activities, *TodaysMeet* engages even the shyest students, because they feel a sense of anonymity even though their names are on the messages they post. Students who might be scared to stand and deliver information in front of peers are typically eager to share it online, because although classmates may be seeing it, the author feels less scrutinized and more anonymous.

Getting Started. Students love *TodaysMeet.com*, because they enjoy conversing online. *TodaysMeet* mimics the social media site, *Twitter*, as each post must be 140 characters or less. Of course, discussion participants can post unlimited responses. Teachers value *TodaysMeet*, because there is no registration required. You simply go to the site and create the URL, or web address, you want for your meeting room. For example, if I teach five class periods daily, I might name a room for a period-one discussion, TodaysMeet.com/Barnes1. I can have students type this into their Internet browser, or I can create a link to it on our classroom website or blog. Students enter the site, type their name, and click, "Join." Another excellent feature of this site for educators is the easy ability to delete information. There is a link called "Delete the room in," followed by a dropdown menu of times, such as "one hour" or "one day," which allows the room administrator to set a time for the created site to disappear. This eliminates any concern teachers may have with students continuing the chat outside of the classroom, when they are not watching. Comparable to blogs, websites, and other social networks, *TodaysMeet* provides one more opportunity for educators to teach their students the value and responsibility of sharing information online. Best of all, it's a powerful way to evaluate learning, without using the multiple-choice bubble tests that most students abhor.

Analyze a Presentation

Upload a slide or a picture or graphic to the website and mobile application, *VoiceThread*, and you can present lessons that stimulate student conversation or allow students to interpret information with presentations of their own. Analogous to the tools mentioned so far, *VoiceThread* empowers all students by giving them a voice. Although the activities, subjects, and grade levels are unlimited, one example might be an art teacher sharing slides that he or she created or slides from the vast libraries that *VoiceThread* provides. Need an activity for tomorrow? Consider this another of the endless options available and possible for any teacher or educator.

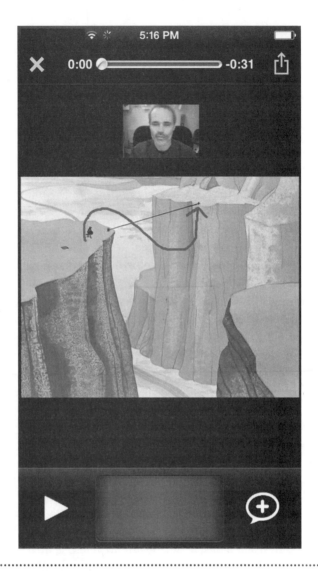

Getting Started. Go to *VoiceThread.com* and create an account. There is the option of opening a K–12 educator account and adding your students, thereby building your own Content Management System, but this is time consuming and unnecessary. Once you are registered, click the "Create" tab, followed by "Upload" and

"Media Sources." From there, click on "New York Public Library" and "Get Digital Images." Choose a collection. (Note that this is ideal for the study of art, but it is also excellent for a language arts or foreign language activity.) For this example, select the collection "Icons and Images of Cultures," then choose the image or images that you want and click the "import" tab at the top. When finished, click "close," and your presentation is ready. Finally, share the presentation with students by getting a link from *VoiceThread* and adding it to the classroom website or just ask students to type the link into their web browsers. Once students access the *VoiceThread* site, they can comment on the slides in a variety of ways, including recording voice observations. They can also draw on the slide, further enhancing their voice or typewritten annotation. When another student or the teacher views each student's comment, any drawing they've done disappears as the viewer moves to the next student's comment. This is another tool and activity with limitless possibilities that can be created in an evening and used in class tomorrow.

Organize a Project

Organization has long been a problem with even the savviest students. Teachers have labored for decades to create and teach organization strategies, especially for lengthy projects with multiple tasks and due dates. The iStudent now has advantages in that arena that most of us could not imagine when we were in school. With websites and apps like *Trello* (a free web-based project management application), planning and organizing projects and other school activities is as easy as type, drag, and drop. Best of all, the student's newly organized plan is not in some agenda book that, in many

> In no time, your students will begin to appreciate the value of planning and finishing tasks, as adding items to a completed list stimulates a sense of accomplishment.

cases, is dropped in a school hallway, or left in a locker, or on a desk in a classroom. *Trello* and similar organization tools (*Todoist* is another) reside in students' pockets or backpacks on their mobile devices. Even if you don't have a current project, you can engage your students with this activity tomorrow.

Getting Started. The *Trello* app is probably most suitable for students starting in third grade and above. If you have a current or upcoming project, this is a perfect chance to help your elementary, middle or high school students plan and organize it. For those with smartphones, iPods, or tablets, have them go to the app store and download *Trello*. Those on a desktop computer can go to *Trello.com*. Depending on their ages, you might want to work through the "How to use Trello" cards with your students. Once they are comfortable with *Trello*'s functions, begin planning a project, activity, or even an entire day. Create a "to-do" card and list a few items. Add a "currently doing" card, and a "finished" card. Instruct students to drag one of the to-do items to the currently doing list and finish that task. When the task is complete, they then drag that task to the finished card. In no time, your students begin to appreciate the value of planning and finishing tasks, as adding items to a completed list stimulates a sense of accomplishment.

If as a teacher you already use web tools and/or mobile apps, your students always appreciate learning about some new technology application. On the other hand, if your students do not get many opportunities to use web tools, they will be overjoyed when they arrive in class tomorrow and you tell them to take out their devices and download something new. I assure you that they will appreciate you as a teacher more, and better yet, this new activity will increase their love of learning.

The Language of "i"

Any fool can write code that a computer can understand.
Good programmers write code that humans can understand.

—*Martin Fowler, software engineer and author*

This chapter isn't about knowing how to write computer code, even though a cursory knowledge of coding is an asset to any 21st-century teacher. Rather, it is about understanding some important technology integration terms that better equip you to teach the iStudent. By no means is this an all-encompassing list; in fact, you may think of words, phrases, or abbreviations that you believe are conspicuously missing. This list covers terms that help me as a teacher of the iStudent, but remember that as time passes, some of them will become obsolete. You can help us keep this list current on the Connected Educators companion website by posting your suggestions and additions. This chapter provides the language of "i" with a list of words, phrases and abbreviations in alphabetical order, to serve as a quick resource whenever needed.

Apps—Applications (apps). The globally recognizable term, apps, refers to web-based or downloadable systems that direct a computer to provide various information and interactive tools to perform useful tasks that can be employed for multiple functions. Although some web tools are referred to as applications, the basic term "app" typically refers to a resource that is downloaded from a web-based store to a mobile device, such as a tablet, an iPod or a smartphone. Google's *Play* and Apple's *iTunes* offer hundreds of thousands of apps for enjoyment, utility, and education. There are thousands of excellent education apps that are free and can be used on multiple devices; many apps also have websites, making them easily accessible on laptops or desktop computers.

AUP—Acceptable Use Policy. The AUP is a formal document, typically signed by students and parents that explains what is and is not acceptable when using computers, mobile devices, and the Internet. Some schools do not have formal AUPs, while others have voluminous AUPs that cover every aspect of technology use, along with student penalties imposed for breaking the rules. Ensuring and teaching acceptable use of technology to students is one of the biggest responsibilities that a 21st-century teacher can face.

Blog—The prior chapter, *Activities and Tools You Can Use Tomorrow*, outlines how a blog functions as a classroom tool, but it's worth adding to this list, since many of your students will not be familiar with the term. Often confused with standard websites, essentially a blog is a web-based journal or diary; however, as the technology has advanced, the blog has evolved into much more than simply a newsletter. The blog host is coded in such a way that it automatically organizes each new page by date, and it can aggregate those pages or blog posts as they are commonly known, into any category that the author chooses. For example, if I write a blog post on iOS devices for the classroom, I might give it categories, or tags, of iPhone, iPad, and iPod. Each time I tag a post with iPad, it is easily located in the iPad category, which can be placed anywhere on the site. The blog can morph into a full-fledged website when static pages are added. Unlike blog posts, the static page does not come with a date and is not categorized. Typical classroom blog pages might be project guidelines, unit pages, or an "About" page, which explains how the entire blog functions. As is true of most of the tools discussed in this book, it is of paramount importance that students realize that blogs are powerful social networking tools, which means that they come with the same learned and acknowledged responsibility for acceptable use as Facebook, Instagram, and the like.

Browser—Web browsers help us navigate the Internet. While most teachers and even many students understand the term "browser," many don't fully grasp the nuances of the various browsers available or, perhaps, the one used by your school district. Popular browsers include Internet Explorer (IE), Mozilla Firefox, Google Chrome, and Safari. It's important to have a cursory understanding of web browsers and to pass this along to students, because the subtle differences can affect what elements you and/or your students require for their activity or project. For example, a video you play at home and intend to share at school may not function at school, depending on which browser the district network uses. Some web applications won't work unless "add-ons" are activated. Add-ons are controlled by the tech people who install the browser on your district's network. Both the teacher and the students need to understand this. All too often, I've seen students work very hard on enhancing a website they were building for a class project, only to be disappointed when a valuable piece failed to materialize in class because of a browser issue.

BYOT/BYOD—Bring Your Own Technology or Bring Your Own Device. In order to supplement increasing textbook costs, many districts, schools, and classrooms are creating a BYOD policy and moving the content to the Internet. Students are encouraged to bring to school mobile devices with Internet capability, such as smartphones, iPods, tablets, and eReaders, thereby putting the ability to find, create, and share information in the palm of their hands. If you are short on computers at your school or class, considering a BYOT policy is critical. Administrators and classroom teachers should create these policies together and be sure to teach them to students. Before you make the transition to a BYOD school or district, be certain to consult and learn from the experiences of other experts and educators who have done so, as there are many considerations. You can't just tell your students one day, "From now on, we'll use devices in class, so bring them daily." Remember, if a few dozen students are using mobile devices, this creates very little pull on your wireless connectivity. If hundreds, or even thousands of students districtwide begin connecting at the same time, and the school does not have the proper bandwidth (network's digital capacity), you may be facing disaster. So, when planning a new BYOD policy, I propose that any school begin with the carpenter's mantra, "Measure twice, cut once."

Cloud computing—While you may not be familiar with this exact vocabulary, you probably know the phrase "in the cloud." Students, especially young ones, often believe that what we create and share on the Internet simply floats in the air—a place we've come to know as cyberspace. Thus, when we tell kids that anything they put on the Internet is "out there" forever, they have a difficult time comprehending this. A perfect way to teach cloud computing is by using Google Drive, Dropbox, or iCloud as examples. These cloud-based platforms come with limits. For most of us, those limits are out of reach, but for someone storing thousands of songs and hundreds of videos, the space can quickly become compact.

The easiest way to explain cloud computing is to tell students that when they create a Google Doc, it is transferred via wireless connection to Google's immense hard drive, or data center. Sure, the document appears to be in the cloud, because it's not stored in a file on a students' network folder. While it may appear to have flown up, up, and away, assure the students that it has not. It's simply being stored on one of Google's thousands of data centers, which are maintained in huge buildings all around the world. This is why retrieving records, for positive or negative reasons, is always easy for people who know how to successfully search for data and want the information badly enough.

EdTech—Short for Education Technology, EdTech is the coined phrase for educators, interested in K–12 technology education. Many people who share education technology websites and tools on Twitter add the hashtag #EdTech.

Embed/embed code—An embed code is nothing more than a piece of computer language (HyperText Markup Language or

HTML) with a clear beginning and ending. The code can be copied and pasted on another website, and it appears exactly as it did in its prior location. This occurs regularly with shared YouTube videos.

Flipped Classroom—The flipped classroom takes a new approach to homework, eliminating most direct instruction and placing it and related concepts in videos for home viewing. The flipped classroom concept has gained traction recently, especially since publication of the book *Flip Your Classroom: Reach Every Student in Every Class Every Day* (Bergmann & Sams, 2012). If you want to try flipping your classroom and sending students home with video instruction, learn how to create your own screen capture videos using a downloadable program like *Jing*, which you can acquire for free at *Techsmith.com*.

Hashtag—I mentioned the hashtag in prior chapters when referring to the social networking service, *Twitter*. A hashtag is any word or phrase with a pound or number sign (#) in front of it. The hashtag aggregates tweets into one stream, creating a conversation on the topic that the hashtag represents. Twitter automatically turns hashtags into web links, so for example, if you ask students to tweet to the hashtag, #fractionmodel, you can click that hashtag's link, and every tweet your students send, including that hashtag, appears on one Twitter page. If you have an interactive whiteboard, you can open the hashtag on Twitter and share it with the entire class. You'll be amazed to see students' faces light up, when they see something they've tweeted come to life on your board.

HTML—Hypertext Markup Language. Although few of your students will become computer programmers, effective digital learning requires a very basic understanding of HTML. For example, all text, graphics, and videos on the Internet have their own HTML. If you and/or your students are creating web pages or blogs, it is important to understand how to retrieve HTML code and properly embed it into your web page. This is much easier than it may sound. If you want to move a YouTube video, for example, you just click "share" under the video, click "embed" and copy the code. Then paste it into your website or blog, using the "text" or "html" editor.

HTTP/ HTTPS—Hypertext Transfer Protocol/ Hypertext Transfer Protocol Secure. Most of your students will never remember what these letters represent (they make for cool *Jeopardy* questions, though), but understanding the use of secure versus unsecure in this context is important. Teach your students that HTTPS indicates that a source is secure. This is important for sites owned by banks, credit card companies, government agencies, and airlines, to name just a few. Teaching students to be on the lookout for security protocols is an important part of teaching acceptable, responsible Internet use.

ISTE—The International Society for Technology in Education. As a teacher of the iStudent, it's important to join organizations like ISTE, which offers a variety of technology resources for educators. The ISTE Annual Conference is one of the biggest EdTech gatherings in the world, providing teachers with a marvelous opportunity to learn about advancements from experts in the field and to discover new tech tools in the vendor section of the conference.

Link—Many students click dozens, perhaps even hundreds, of web links daily, yet they may not truly comprehend the term "link." Be sure students understand that "link" can be both a noun and a verb. Clicking on a link (noun form) opens a new site. If you instruct a student to "Link that page to your blog," this is a verb form. Knowing the grammar may be irrelevant, but understanding the difference is important. Unlike a URL (uniform resource locator), or web address, which begins with the letters *http* or *www* (World Wide Web), a link is usually a word or phrase, which masks the URL. Poll your students on this, and you'll be amazed by just how few understand URLs and links.

Navigation—When explaining navigation, I tell students that it is simply moving from one place to another within a website, blog, or other place on the Internet. Some websites have thousands of pages. It's important to teach students the various navigation options on a site, such as top navigation, side navigation, and links within a site and how these work. After a few years, my classroom website had hundreds of pages, filled with project guidelines, embedded videos, pictures, assessments, and vast libraries of web links to outside resources. Some menu tabs contained hierarchical trees, with each branch leading to a valuable, related subpage. These hierarchies can be very confusing for inexperienced users. Teaching students how to navigate these vast forests is a necessary part of any digitally enhanced classroom.

NETS—Developed by ISTE (the International Society for Technology in Education), NETS are The National Education Technology Standards. The NETS are designed to help educators set standards of excellence in teaching with technology. ISTE created a separate set of NETS for students and educators. For more information about the NETS, visit the Connected Educators companion website.

PLN—Personal Learning Network/Professional Learning Network. A PLN is created using various social media, such as *Twitter*, *Facebook*, *LinkedIn*, and *Pinterest*. The concept is to build a network of people locally, regionally, and globally that provides both conversation and resources to help you improve personally and professionally. The PLN is an important tool for content curation. Teach your students to use a PLN to gather knowledge that they can maintain in places like blogs and their own social media. Be sure to explain how they can use this amazing network to enhance their learning—from any place, at any time.

URL—Uniform Resource Locator. Most people come to understand this as the specific web address that is typed into a web browser and points to a website. Knowing what URL stands for might be helpful in a game of Trivial Pursuit; otherwise, it's not powerful information, but it is worth sharing with students.

Wiki—A wiki is a website host that allows users to collaborate on a single web page. Wikis are known for "What-You-See-Is-What-You-Get" editors (WYSIWYG), meaning HTML is not needed. Wikis are excellent for projects, because students can work together in the same onsite location, much like Google Drive.

Remember, this is a living, growing list. Teachers are never finished helping the iStudent learn the vocabulary of the web, so use this and the companion website as go-to resources.

Conclusion

What's the Internet?

I n October of 1996, I was partnered with three wonderful teachers on an academic team at a middle school outside of Cleveland, Ohio. Long before interdisciplinary projects were popular, two of my brilliant colleagues suggested that we have our students work in groups of three or four on a project we later named, "I Dream a World." Students were to colonize a planet or moon in our solar system. They needed to calculate travel time from the Earth to their planet along with the dimensions of their colonies (math). A written charter and constitution were necessary, along with promotional material for their new world (social studies and language arts). Finally, students needed an intimate understanding of their planet or moon, its terrain, distance from the Earth as well as other facts (science).

A wealth of information had to be presented and absorbed by about 90 young minds. "There's a lot of research here," I observed one day, as the four of us planned the project over lunch. "Won't we need a lot of library time?" Little did I know that another colleague, a computer teacher, was listening and had an idea that would have never occurred to me, prior to that day.

"We can have them search for much of the information on the Internet," she said.

"What's the Internet?" I asked.

In the days and weeks thereafter, I observed our students carefully, as they feverishly sought information, using the search engine *AltaVista* (Larry Page and Sergey Brin had yet to launch *Google*). I was astonished with the results. A boy typed the word "Jupiter" into the search field and perhaps a few dozen website links appeared, far from the more than 9 million available when searching for that same term on Google today. This approach to learning was so new that we weren't even certain how to teach it. Yet, our students learned more in a few weeks of locating information about our solar system using the Internet, than they could have in several years of in-class text work and teacher lecture. Assisted by the newfound power of the Internet, our students produced work that received local media attention, and their teachers were even invited to present the project at the National Middle School Principals Conference.

Not long ago, I reminisced about those days with three of the teachers I worked with on that project, including the one in charge of our lone computer lab. "That was the dawn of web-based instruction," I said. "We had no idea where we were headed." It occurred to me at that very moment, before I even started outlining this book, that back then, almost 20 years ago, the iStudent was born. He didn't use an iPod or iPhone, but he did use the Internet—an amazing, powerful new tool that would forever change teaching and learning.

Now decades later, as I alluded to in Chapter 1, the speed at which the technology is moving is almost frightening. AltaVista, once arguably the most popular search engine in the world, was shut down in the summer of 2013, no longer able to compete with the powerhouse Google search engine (Lee, 2013). The computers that were once so large that they needed an entire room are now infinitely faster, complete millions more tasks, contain far more information and, most astoundingly, fit in the palm of your hand. Back in the days of AltaVista and the limited results it returned, it would have taken a Star Trek-type visionary to predict the impact that computers and the Internet would have on information. As shocking as it is that the search engine is less than 20 years old, social networks are still children, existing for only half as long as Google. Yet, ask your students or even your colleagues where they learned of a recent news event or interesting fact or where they saw that funny video, and they will undoubtedly say *Facebook*, *Twitter*, or *YouTube*.

The Internet, social media, and electronic devices are fascinating entertainers that hypnotize our students every day, transforming them into iStudents. These digital natives come fully equipped with mobile learning tools and just enough know-how to be dangerous, both figuratively and literally speaking.

Just like newborns need mothers to meet their needs, iStudents need iTeachers. As their parents show them how to walk, talk, and tie their shoes, the iTeacher must teach them to harness the power at their fingertips and become the next generation of Internet-savvy independent learners who will most certainly reshape the world as we know it.

References

Barnes, M. (2013a). *Role reversal: Achieving uncommonly excellent results in the student-centered classroom.* Alexandria: ASCD.

Barnes, M. (2013b). *The 5-minute teacher: How do I maximize time for learning in my classroom?* Alexandria: ASCD.

Bergmann, J., & Sams, A. (2012). *Flip your classroom: Reach every student in every class every day.* Alexandria, VA: Association for Supervision and Curriculum Development (ASCD).

Donahoo, D. (2012, February 13). *Curating children's content: Who is doing it, and why?* [Web log post]. Retrieved from http://www.wired.com/geek dad/2012/02/curating-childrens-content/

Harris Interactive. (2013, April 5). *Pearson student mobile device survey 2013. National report: Students in grades 4–12.* Retrieved from http://www .pearsoned.com/wp-content/uploads/Pearson-Student-Mobile-Device-Survey-2013-National-Report-on-Grades-4-to-12-public-release.pdf

Henley, J. (2013, August 6). *Ask.fm: Is there a way to make it safe?* Retrieved from http://www.theguardian.com/society/2013/aug/06/askfm-way-to-make-it-safe

Johnson, D. (2014, February). Power up! Why Facebook belongs in your school. *Educational Leadership, 71*(5), 82–83.

Klock, G. (2011, January 11). *Teachers vs. cell phones: Mobile devices win.* Retrieved from http://elearnmag.acm.org/featured.cfm?aid=1925038

Lee, T. (2013, July 11). *AltaVista is dead. Here's why it is so hard to compete with Google* [Web log message]. Retrieved from http://www.washingtonpost .com/blogs/wonkblog/wp/2013/07/11/altavista-is-dead-heres-why-its-so-hard-to-compete-with-google/

Meredith, L. (2012, September 11). More teens using smartphones; are they hand-me-downs? Retrieved from *NBCNews Technology* at http://www .nbcnews.com/technology/more-teens-using-smartphones-are-they-hand-me-downs-992817

Mitrano, T. (2013, May 31). *Moocs as a lightening rod* [Web log message]. Retrieved from http://www.insidehighered.com/blogs/law-policy-and-it/ moocs-lightning-rod

Moss, P. (2013, November 26). [Web log message]. *Why learning through social networks is the future.* Retrieved from http://www.teachthought .com/technology/learning-through-networks-is-the-future/

National Governors Association Center for Best Practices & Council of Chief State School Officers. (2010). *Common Core State Standards for Mathematics.* Washington, DC: Authors.

O'Connell, J. (2012, March 12). Educators as content curators [Web log post]. Retrieved from *HeyJude: Learning in an online world* at http://judyoconnell.com/2012/03/12/educators-as-content-curators/

Rainie, L. (2011, October 20). *As learning goes mobile.* Retrieved from Pew Internet and American Life Project at http://www.pewinternet.org/Presentations/2011/Oct/Educase-2011.aspx

Sterling, G. (2013, May 21). *Pew: 94% of teenagers use Facebook, have 425 Facebook friends but Twitter & Instagram adoption way up.* Retrieved from http://marketingland.com/pew-the-average-teenager-has-425-4-facebook-friends-44847

CORWIN

A SAGE Company

The Corwin logo—a raven striding across an open book—represents the union of courage and learning. Corwin is committed to improving education for all learners by publishing books and other professional development resources for those serving the field of PreK–12 education. By providing practical, hands-on materials, Corwin continues to carry out the promise of its motto: **"Helping Educators Do Their Work Better."**